The
Little Book
of
Peace

The
Little Book
of
Peace

Finding tranquillity in a troubled world

TIDDY ROWAN

piatkus

PIATKUS

First published in Great Britain in 2016 by Piatkus

Extract by Dr Scilla Elworthy, 2015. Reproduced with permission.
Extract by Doc Childre and Howard Martin from The HeartMath Institute, 2016.
Reproduced with permission.
Extract from Thich Nhat Hanh, *A Handful of Quiet*. Reproduced with permission.
Extract from Bertrand Russell Peace Foundation, 1963. Reproduced with permission.
Extract by Education International, 2014. Reproduced with permission.

Typeset in Century by M Rules
Printed and bound in Great Britain by Clays Ltd, St Ives plc

Papers used by Piatkus are from well-managed forests
and other responsible sources.

MIX
Paper from
responsible sources
FSC
www.fsc.org FSC® C104740

Piatkus
An imprint of
Little, Brown Book Group
Carmelite House
50 Victoria Embankment
London EC4Y 0DZ

An Hachette UK Company
www.hachette.co.uk

www.improvementzone.co.uk

Introduction

I went to Paris in November to spend a peaceful week relaxing after a busy work spell. I wanted to wander around some galleries, see friends and most of all sit on café pavements to watch the world go by and to think some new thoughts.

The apartment where I was staying was in the Marais, a fifteen-minute walk from the Bataclan theatre. I had just come back in after meeting a friend for a drink and I switched on the television to watch the news – the news I had not yet heard. The brutal massacre at the theatre and nearby cafés was being reported on television, in real time. I could hear the same sirens through my open window, as the ambulances and emergency services raced towards the stricken areas that Friday night, where a hundred and thirty innocent people died and more than three hundred and fifty were wounded.

Saturday was a day of aftershock. Most of Paris stayed inside – dealing with their grief or outrage. One old man at the otherwise empty supermarket told me it reminded him of Paris under siege during the war.

Sunday was a bright sunny day, which contrasted with the sadness, the grief and the disbelief. I met friends for lunch on the Île Saint-Louis in the centre of Paris. We ate outside at a pavement table; we walked in the sunshine among the usual throng of people enjoying a beautiful city – but one that had been so viciously wounded two days earlier. At dusk we joined thousands of people for a vigil outside the Notre Dame cathedral, where the ancient bells tolled for the recently dead.

In the days that followed, I was struck by a sense of shared defiance on the streets. People passing acknowledged one another with a look, a brief smile, a nod ... as though commiserating in peaceful camaraderie. The united strength was palpable and impressive in the face of terror.

I did sit in cafés and meet with friends, but my thoughts had now turned to how peace could come from terror; the importance of holding on to our own inner peace and strength in the face of adversity and how so many Parisians, and world citizens, were thinking the same thing.

I started to think of different aspects of peace, and the importance of making the connection between our inner peace of mind and the outer peace of the world. Since each of us is connected with the world and all the events that trigger or threaten our peace, it is important, it seemed to me, to open our eyes and senses to the world around us. Our relationships with other people, on whatever level – family, friendships, work – are ultimately connected to our inner peace and vice versa, so that our lives are one continuous interaction with the world.

Neither words nor an ideal can comfort the loss of someone close in unpeaceful circumstances – in that moment. In order for the words not to remain merely ideological, though, I believe it is within all of us to increase our own levels of peacefulness and, through understanding and compassion, make a contribution to developing a more peaceful world.

I resolved to research peace in all its hues and to glean insights from experts and thinkers on how to conduct our internal and external worlds so that we may find ways of bridging the gap between the two. I resolved, too, to discover how we can strive to live a more peaceful existence despite, or even because of, the odds so often stacked against it.

Tiddy Rowan
May 2016

'Peace is not simply the absence of war; it is a virtue, a state of mind, a disposition for benevolence, confidence and justice.'

SPINOZA

States of peace:

To be in a personal element of freedom from anxiety, unnecessary concerns, noise or unwanted confrontation.

For communities, countries and the world to be free from war, violence and aggressive conflict.

To be at peace with the world, we must first be at peace with ourselves ...

For any hope of outer peace it is essential to develop inner peace; to embark on a committed journey towards attaining peacefulness; to 'practise' it daily. If the commitment is whole-hearted, positive results will emanate. Even if we start by making one peaceful contribution in a day – it could be solving a quarrel between children, in resisting an unnecessary argument with someone, in positively thinking about peace in a quiet period of meditation or mindfulness – that is a lot of peace-making in a year. Each act of peace is a positive contribution towards a more harmonious world.

'Life is really simple, but we insist on making it complicated.'

CONFUCIUS

Confucius was a teacher and philosopher (551 BCE–479 BCE), admired chiefly for his everyday common sense and natural human qualities. The following is a passage taken from a primary lesson for children, and one that makes as good a teaching in education today as it did when he wrote it.

*'The ancient people who desired to have a clear
moral harmony in the world would first order
their national life; those who desired to order
their national life would first regulate their home
life; those who desired to regulate their home
life would first cultivate their personal lives;
those who desired to cultivate their personal
lives would first set their hearts right; those
who desired to set their hearts right would first
make their wills sincere; those who desired to
make their wills sincere would first arrive at
understanding; understanding comes from the
exploration of knowledge of things.*

*When the knowledge of things is gained, then
understanding is reached; when understanding
is reached, then the will is sincere; when the
will is sincere, then the heart is set right; when
the heart is set right, then the personal life is
cultivated; when the personal life is cultivated,
then the home life is regulated; when the home life
is regulated, then the national life is orderly; and
when the national life is orderly: then the world is
at peace.'*

CONFUCIUS

I love the simplicity of Confucius' writing in tackling a subject often so fraught with contradiction, misinterpretation, conflict and elusiveness. But he manages to make it accessible, straightforward, easy almost, and well within our grasp.

So we in turn can recognise this need to develop and nurture inner peace, peace between ourselves and those we live with, our families, our close friends, our community, our environment, our country ... and our world.

Peace is not a lofty illusion, nor does it have to be embraced in the name of religion – it is a simple, secular, human attribute, something we can all practise, every day, irrespective of our personal spiritual beliefs. Imagine the cumulative energy if everyone were participating in the *attitude* as well as the activity? Then an invisible shield would fortify us. We have a desire to be united, at some level, with those we choose to have around us, and we are strengthened by that link. If this unity is reinforced with a determination for peace and resistance to conflict, then a renewed collective strength will develop.

'Our work for peace must begin within the private world of each of us. To build for man a world without fear, we must be without fear. To build a world of justice, we must be just.'

DAG HAMMARSKJOLD

Fear is a great deterrent to peace – and the strongest card that an aggressor holds. In overcoming fear, we diffuse the bully's – or persecutor's – method of control and coercion.

Let peaceful minds become the deterrent to fear, not the other way round.

Peace of mind is not the absence of conflict in life,
but the ability to cope with it.

To instantly calm a fearful mind, focus on your breathing.

Focus on counting to four as you breathe in, hold it for four and count to four as you breathe out. Choose another number to count up to and back again if it makes you more comfortable. The importance is in concentrating on your breathing. Counting the breaths in this way is an aid to that concentration. As the breaths gradually slow down naturally they take longer to flow in and out, finding their own, more relaxed pace. Your whole body and mind will follow suit and a sense of peace and strength will be restored.

Tips for dispelling fear.

- Work out exactly what it is you are afraid of – and why.

- Being fearful is often to do with not being in control of a situation.

- Learn to let go of the need to control and fear will become diffused.

- Practise relaxation techniques – fear is up there with stress.

- Practise meditation, mindfulness or simple breathing exercises.

- Keep things in perspective. Balance the unknown with the known and focus on the present moment.

- Develop a more positive outlook on aspects of your life, starting with what you are grateful for, and gradually widen that positive outlook on a daily basis.

- When you have fearful thoughts, simply change your mind. Choose to think about something else.

- Be selective about how much news you watch. Much of it is media sensation to attract viewers, and distressing images can, as we know, forge themselves into our subconscious. We need to maintain a balance between knowing enough about world events to be informed, but not so overloaded with them that it causes us anxiety about things we cannot change.

- Remember: the choice is ours. To fear or not to fear.

Relaxation tips.

- If possible, remove yourself from what's causing you a feeling of stress. The very act of redirecting your attention takes your mind away from what is causing the anxiety.

- Distract yourself by reading a book, a newspaper or a magazine (do something physical, i.e. not looking at a screen).

- Put on some dance music and dance freely. Even dancing for two minutes shakes up our cluttered minds.

- Listen to a piece of music as though you were the arranger in a recording studio – concentrate on the different instruments or voice, and the pace, the beat, the rhythm and how the overall piece makes you feel.

A relaxation exercise.

- Sit or lie comfortably but not in a sleep-inducing position. You want to be fully relaxed without falling asleep.

- Keep the spine in alignment. If you are sitting, don't lean against the back of the chair but sit upright with the shoulders dropped, the knees uncrossed and together, with the feet flat on the ground. Have good posture, but not stiff.

- Let all tension out of your body. Keep the muscles relaxed not tensed.

- Observe particularly the muscles in the face, the forehead, the temples, around the eyes, the nose and mouth, the jaw and the neck.

- By thinking of each area in turn you can feel the tension leaving the muscles.

- Continue through the body being aware of the muscles by flexing them individually and then relaxing them.

Fear is usually associated with the anticipation of something that hasn't actually happened. When we are in the face of real danger or confrontation we have little time to be fearful since we switch to a fight, flight or negotiation mode, an instinctive reaction with the right dose of naturally provided adrenalin.

Next time you are fearful, remember ... it is a state of mind for something that hasn't happened and therefore might not happen. Instead, use the time to turn fear to awareness of being fully present in the moment. Be proactive and worry less about what might not happen.

'Nobody can hurt me without my permission.'

MAHATMA GANDHI

The one constant in our lives is change. Nothing stays the same. Both in times of despair and in times of great happiness, it is good to reflect on this inconstant constant. When anything reaches either its peak or its nadir, it is, at that point, about to change direction. We only have to see the sun at midday or the moon at its fullest to know that it is already on its descent, or its waning. To go with the flow and the pace of nature is to stay mindful of a peaceful centre; to be able to enjoy the good times but not despair in the midst of difficult ones.

Keeping a steady pendulum.

In the same way that a pendulum in motion finds its diametric opposite, so events also have a natural inclination towards their opposite. The harder you push the pendulum, the further it travels in its swing to the opposite. So it is with events in our lives. The cycle of life is one of constant movement – of loss and gain, of destruction and healing, decrease and growth, of discord and harmony. It is good to meditate on this, to keep us in balance and remind us that if peace eludes us – whether because of a quarrel, or physical pain or depression – as long as we have made a place for peace in our lives, peace will return.

Balance.

However stormy the sea or loud the thunder, the seas will calm and the skies will clear. We know this from observing the movement of the clouds and the changes in the weather. This is a good analogy for life, since we are, essentially, all elements of the same universe which turns on the mystery of balance; the same balance that we need in our bodies on a physical level, and in our minds and souls on a spiritual one.

'There is peace even in the storm.'

Do you want stress in your life, or peace? Do you want to be in a relationship where there is constant tension and fighting, or do you want to have fun, be loved and loving in a happy rhythm with your partner and friends? Would you like to live in a harmonious home or a discordant one? Do you want your neighbourhood to be a peaceful one, or a troubled one? And wouldn't we all prefer to live in a world where peace prospers? Do you see how peace is embodied in the answers to most of these questions? And we have the choice – to contribute to peace or not. It is up to each one of us, each individual, to generate strength through peace, to instigate peace, to choose peaceful means over conflict or quarrel.

Keep peace simple. 'Be' peaceful now. See how, by focusing on it as a desired way of being, you can alter your mindset. It is akin to letting the shoulders drop, releasing tension from the body and taking a few steady breaths, bringing the *value* of peace to join in with the breathing. At its most basic form it is, quite simply, the only way forward.

There is no future in waiting. Start now. Smile at the next person you encounter and take it on from there.

The word 'peace' sometimes has cumbersome connotations. It can become entangled with the thornier aspects of religion, tradition and duty. The word is used in playgrounds and classrooms as well as political salons; it is bartered with in treaties while also forming a greeting between people on a path to enlightenment. So it is hardly surprising that the word itself can get in the way. We need to be selective in using the word as we want it to mean – be that harmony, tranquillity, stillness or silence, relaxation, quiet, reconciliation, truce, unity, a salutation or farewell, absence of violence or confrontation, or personal serenity. These are words to think about in quiet moments so that we can get closer to creating whichever frame of mind we want or need.

'All speech,' said the anthropologist Dr Franz Uri Boas, (1858–1942) 'is intended to serve for the communication of ideas.' Most of us talk 'automatically', but when it comes to discussion or communication that transmits our 'peaceful' code of behaviour, we need to choose our words especially carefully. Body language and facial expressions further endorse the meaning of our words. We need to be mindful of our body language – since it can contradict the meaning of our words, as well as confirm it.

Body language.

When we cannot use language to communicate, we resort to universal signs that come naturally to indicate hunger, tiredness, fear, happiness, a welcome or a dismissal.

In our everyday communication we may use subconscious signals to accompany verbal exchange. We can pick up meaning from these signals, though it's not always helpful to attach a fixed interpretation. For example, someone folding their arms in front of them may not be doing so out of defensiveness, it might simply be a comfortable position, or because they are feeling the cold or expressing a pensive attitude.

However, we can be aware of the signals that *we* send out ourselves – consciously. If we want to endorse our peaceful or compassionate intentions then we can select our own non-verbal language through eye expression (a softening of the eyes as distinct from a hard stare), through non-clenched fists, through facial expressions of smile or non-clenched jaw or mouth ... We can easily find what these are by practising different gestures and seeing what feelings we are aware of conveying.

The very *act* of being peaceful, thinking peacefully, eradicating fear, does not need to have a label. With the right mindset there is nothing intrinsically difficult about accessing or practising peace. In fact, it is often easier to attain than, say, the complexity of love or happiness as a concept, once we become aware of how it can start changing our lives for the better.

Having a vision of what we want in our lives.

Sometimes when we feel a lack of inner peace it's because we have lost sight of, or haven't decided what we want in our lives. Not a fantasy longing, but a real idea of the person we want to be. It isn't necessarily enough to meditate or use mindfulness to empty the mind. It is important to also use the quiet, still time to let the inner person come through.

Having a positive mental picture of being a whole and healthy person is in itself a manageable aspiration that gives us a constructive framework. Each of us will have a different vision of what that important framework is, what is most vital for us to achieve within our abilities (or possibly beyond them), as long as it allows us to be at peace with ourselves. Perhaps that is an aspiration that we all share fundamentally – to be at peace – and can meditate on how we can best achieve it.

And what happens when we don't have a vision in our lives? We become scattered and less clear as to what our own private core values are if they are not in some way hinged to who we are and how we want to be or what we want to become.

Spend time working out what constitutes a peaceful life for yourself.

Once we know what it is we are seeking, it is easier to find.

The new day ...

Anyone who has ever slept under the stars in open countryside will surely recognise the sense of peace experienced by Robert Louis Stevenson in the following passage from his book *Travels With a Donkey in the Cévennes* (1879). Observing the first new day as he awoke from sleeping outdoors, he marvels at the change in the sky from dark to light, from night to day, from nocturnal thoughts to morning revelations.

'Day was at hand. I lit my lantern, and by its glow-worm light put on my boots and gaiters; then I broke up some bread for Modestine [his donkey], filled my can at the water-tap, and lit my spirit lamp to boil myself some chocolate. The blue darkness lay long in the glade where I had so sweetly slumbered; but soon there was a broad streak of orange melting into gold along the mountain-tops of Vivarais. A solemn glee possessed my mind at this gradual and lovely coming in of day. I heard the runnel with delight; I looked round me for something beautiful and unexpected; but the still black pine-trees, the hollow glade, the munching ass, remained unchanged in figure. Nothing had altered but the light, and that, indeed, shed over all a spirit of life and of breathing peace, and moved me to a strange exhilaration.'*

ROBERT LOUIS STEVENSON, *Travels With a Donkey in the Cévennes* (1879)

If we're lucky, we can share in the experience by spending a couple of days in the open countryside or near the sea. Try to sleep with the curtain or blinds open so that you wake gently pre-dawn. Best of all, at this point go outside and savour that exhilaration, which will surely come from the next hour spent watching the light change and the sun come up. Find times to sleep out under the stars, weather permitting, to enjoy the full experience through all the senses.

Sleeping under the stars may sound like a far cry from images we see on the evening news, but keeping a sense of balance in our lives is part of what keeps us grounded in the face of adversity and strengthens our peaceful core.

Being merged with the scale of nature affords us the space to recognise the resources that are there within us to help resolve our problems or face difficulties. It is often not until we return to our day-to-day activities that we are aware of this renewed strength and energy.

The new day is also vital in giving us a fresh start – every day. No matter how difficult the day before might have been, or how turbulent the night, there is always renewed hope with the new day; a new chance, a new beginning. Instead of taking the new day for granted, or starting it grudgingly, we should really value it and be grateful for another opportunity to start afresh.

In the few moments after waking, put the night behind you and think about the day ahead. Not so much the diary schedule itself but what you want to achieve from the day in your personal development ... how you want to be and what adjustments you might want to make in order to reach that achievement. Make an intention. It might be that you want to feel more peaceful and less agitated, or by focusing on the importance of tranquillity in your life you will attempt to have good relations with people by being aware of their needs as well as your own. By acknowledging that thought, whatever the intention is, really being aware of it, it will filter through to our deeper awareness as well as our conscious resolve. It doesn't have to be overly complicated – it is as though we are simply setting the tone for the day, which is achievable.

Even in a hurried world it takes no time to adjust the mind from night mode to day. It needs only a moment of awareness and focus in which to make a conscious decision to switch off the night and face the new day with equanimity, to be strong in the face of adversity, to be patient with other people.

Think: positive, patient, peaceful.

In order to get the best out of the new day, allow time after waking to get up peacefully. Most of us hit the snooze button in order to get ten minutes more sleep, but if we need to get more focus in our life in general and the day ahead in particular, that extra half an hour is better spent on a combination of meditation, mindfulness or exercise of some sort.

However busy you are, most people can organise getting up half an hour earlier, despite the initial resistance. It may take adjustment, possibly even meaning going to bed half an hour earlier, depending on how much sleep you need, but you will be amazed at how quickly it becomes natural and how soon you will feel the benefits of it.

That early hour is quieter and probably the most peaceful time of the day. Practise a combination of meditation or mindfulness for 10–15 minutes followed by 15 minutes of stretches, yoga, pilates or exercises – or a combination of whatever works for you. During the time of simply sitting still your meditation can be either focusing on the breathing, emptying the mind ready for the day's input or visualising the changes and success that you are going to achieve in the day.

Before leaving the house, when you're gathering up your keys and phone, spend a moment consciously putting peace in your pocket. It could be a smooth pebble or anything small that you can keep in your pocket, just something that is symbolic of being peaceful when you make contact with it.

'Peace begins with a smile.'

MOTHER TERESA

Developing inner peace strengthens us in the face of danger. If we are confronted by a physical attack we have to protect ourselves the best we can. We have to know when to fight our corner. Faced with conflict, emotional exploitation, business plots or conspiracies is no time to show weakness, but to show strength and resilience. Which is why practising some form of meditation or mindfulness is helpful in sharpening our instincts, developing awareness and being alert to changes in circumstances. Having a strong core of inner peace provides a place to return to, to fortify us and protect us.

Practising t'ai chi and qigong is good exercise, strengthens our internal force and gives us confidence. T'ai chi, a graceful and slow-moving exercise, or 'dance', develops not only the inner 'qi' or life force but also teaches the basic movements for self-defence.

It may seem like a contradiction to talk about practising some form of fighting art or self-defence while exercising peaceful conduct, but the key here is *de*fence not *of*fence.

Moving east to west, some 2,500 years after Confucius.

In 1963, the British philosopher and peace activist Bertrand Russell, preoccupied by the threat of nuclear war, launched his Peace Foundation.

It was established in order to carry forward Russell's work for peace, human rights and social justice.

'The Foundation was formed to further the cause of peace, and to assist in the pursuit of freedom and justice. It sought to identify and counter the causes of violence, and to identify and oppose the obstacles to worldwide community. It was designed to promote research into disarmament, wars and threats of war, and to publish the results. It has consistently laboured to carry on the work of its founder in a spirit of fidelity to the standards of reason and tolerance, which he [Bertrand Russell] did so much to advance. Accordingly, it has always struggled for freedom of thought and opinion, and for non-exploitative forms of human association.'

PEACE FOUNDATION AIMS

There is strength, not weakness, in peace.

'Today the real test of power is not the capacity to make war but the capacity to prevent it.'

ANNE O'HARE MCCORMICK

With an increase in awareness and mindfulness in the world today, it is interesting to see that the people with good business skills who are also kind, considerate and compassionate towards others are those who are winning accounts and sales. People prefer customer service providers who are humanly agreeable, and so it is on up through the job chain. CEOs and tycoons display philanthropy in their keenness to show compassion to those less fortunate, hungry or poor. In big businesses, classes teaching mindfulness are incorporated into the working day to help alleviate stress and encourage a more peaceful mindset.

When considering how we come across to other people, remember we are not considering how we come across *compared* to other people but how we are in ourselves. We must decide how to make the best of what we have – not just physically but in our values and in our behaviour towards others. Finding that balance, being the best of 'ourselves', leads on to confidence and helps to generate harmonious relationships.

We're all going to grow old some day – if we're lucky. Maybe growing old peacefully is part of growing old gracefully. If we manage to develop peace of mind and live our lives consciously, with awareness, the better our chances will be of being equipped for any vicissitudes of growing old. A key factor with many older people is enjoying their memories, so it is important that we store up good times and experiences to savour later. Being able to 'tell our story' to ourselves is the foundation of our memories, when we will be able to savour the richer morsels from our banquet of life whenever we like. People who have trouble connecting to their memories or integrating them into their lives are very often the ones who are lonelier in later life.

Having patience and tolerance towards older people is showing compassion. It's easy to forget that we may well be that old person one day. By improving our own peace of mind through compassion, we are enabling other people to have peace of mind as well.

Tips to strengthen our peace and compassion core.

- Relax more.

- Listen to other people. Really listen to what they're saying.

- Focus your attention on the other person.

- Be kind.

- Be patient.

- Laugh more – keep a sense of humour.

- After an argument with someone you love, be the first to say sorry.

- Don't dwell on things. Move on.

- Keep calm.

- Be generous, share what you have.

- Offer to shake hands with people (at meetings, introductions, etc).

- The outstretched hand is symbolic of extending the hand of peace.

'You cannot shake hands with a clenched fist.'

INDIRA GANDHI

Developing a compassionate attitude helps in times of conflict. For example, when an argument flares up we are already better positioned to handle it. Two key factors in solving a quarrel are: a) to find out what the other party wants or would like to happen, and b) to give some indication that we *have* heard, that we *have* listened. This is enough to open the way for negotiation and reconciliation. Simply by adjusting our own attitude and actions, we can bring back some balance into the situation. We cannot control other people, or their minds, but their minds *might* change as a *result* of our own, ongoing, peace habits.

What is important is the application. For example, it is the difference between reading a book of instructions and actually carrying them out.

Peace is not just for resolving conflict. Peace will only come into our lives if we want it to. And if we do, then gradually, through practical gestures, our lives and our relationships, our work output, our happiness and our equanimity are stabilised into a firmer foundation to deal with conflicts when they do arise.

Very often we overlook our own deep-down intentions. We become accustomed to reciting a litany of what we want or think we need in some particular order, like a list that is in some way doable by virtue of being a list. This can become unwieldy since once we are in this mindset the list becomes too big to handle – a better job, a house to live in, the right partner, constant good health ... and so on. But fundamentally, when we pare it back to one overall aspiration that would in turn start to *make* everything else fall into place, very often those aspirations are relatively attainable. We want good health? Then we must address what adjustments we may need to make. We want to love and be loved? Are we ready for this as we are or do we need to make a few self-improvements first in order to maximise our love potential?

And if we want inner peace and genuine happiness? Then we need to make room for this to take root and blossom. We can't just wish for it and leave it at that. We need to make a real connection with the aspiration, an awareness that we hold on to so that it becomes a deep and genuine application.

By practising an openness, an awareness and a commitment to loving kindness towards ourselves and humanity – towards all sentient beings – we can be sure that it is a way of opening up a channel for joy and peace to enter our lives.

We are in this for the long haul. If we become dispirited because of a setback, or abandon the practice of peace too soon because of frustration, then we cannot expect the positive results we initially set out to achieve.

There will be days, spells even, when we lose the thread, lose touch with the original energy of our enterprise. That's when we have to hold firm, wait for the storm to pass and continue our journey.

At the very least, bookending each day with a resolve in the morning and a reflection in the evening will keep the thread of awareness going, even if we have had a difficult or challenging day.

If we can achieve peace of mind we will be happy whether or not we have wealth, possessions or power – even love and good health; if we lack peace of mind we can never be truly happy, whatever our circumstances in life. So our starting point, and our point of return when we lose our way, is always nourishing our well of inner peace and strength.

What is the healthiest way to achieve well-being, serenity, confidence and strength in your life? Focus on what is important to you and work outwards towards what you are able to achieve in the world. We have to go right to the core – to the centre of our being – in order to start any worthwhile journey.

If we don't manage to maintain an inner stability of peace then constant and often conflicting messages are confusing. We become pulled in different directions either by outside influences or our own unsettled views or ambitions. Developing the practice of returning to our authentic self through some form of meditation, mindfulness or contemplation on a regular basis will strengthen that core and we will see how, by cultivating a peaceful disposition, our lives will gradually change for the better. We will make decisions more effectively, hear our inner voice more distinctly, become less anxious and be strengthened with self-confidence.

For people who find it difficult to sit still in contemplation – initially – there are activities that are akin to meditation. Learning a skill in creating pottery, painting, making bread, playing a musical instrument. In fact, any creative craft that involves using our hands occupies our focus on what we are doing and allows the mind to rest in a neutral and tranquil place. Which is why spending time surrounded by nature or even in a small patch of town garden puts us in a better frame of mind and spirit. People who are bed-bound or chair-bound, through ill health or physical hindrance because of old age, are consistent in their appreciation of having a window through which they can see the sky, watch the clouds, and see the birds, or have a tree or garden to look at and become immersed in nature – albeit through a window. How much luckier are those of us who can freely wander outside, go on a hike, take up gardening or develop a creative skill by which to ease our minds and spirits?

But meditation dedicated to sitting still and quietly in a chair is pretty much available to us all, and the most direct route to creating the basis, the foundation, of inner quiet from which inner peace can grow and thrive.

How to fit it into your busy life, though? Don't be overwhelmed by the idea that meditation is complicated, obscure, something that other people do or something that you might get round to giving a try – but 'not now', when you have 'more time'. Busy people rarely have 'more time' unless they make room for it. Essentially, it's up to us how we prioritise what is important and to manage our time accordingly.

'Whoever values peace of mind and the health of the soul will live the best of all possible lives.'

MARCUS AURELIUS

If you told people that they could be financially richer by just spending half an hour a day, or every few days, filling in a form, they would almost certainly do it. It's no different with our spiritual or well-being currency. The increase in personal peace and all that is derived from meditation or mindfulness is ours for that extra time input. Once you have touched that well of peace and inner security you will not be making any time sacrifices, you will find the space and time eagerly.

As for the complexity of meditation or contemplation, there really isn't any. Certainly, religious monks may appear to be preoccupied by meditation for much of the day, but that is because it's their life. For us in the outside world, we are looking for a way of incorporating meditation to suit our own lives, in helping overcome anxiety and inner turmoil. If, as a result, the mind starts to become quieter and less confused by daily situations, then it is a turning point. The power of peace is under way.

*'My greatest wealth is the deep stillness in which
I strive and grow and win what the world cannot
take from me with fire and sword.'*

JOHANN WOLFGANG VON GOETHE

When we are bombarded with feelings of being over-whelmed, we need to be able to access help quickly and easily – like having an energy drink to hand just when you need it. Professor Mark Williams formulated just such a booster in his MBCT (Mindfulness Based Cognitive Therapy) course. He sees it as an 'emergency meditation' that allows you to be aware, moment to moment, when you feel under pressure; to manage the pause in your thoughts before they spiral out of control and to keep a sense of perspective to reground yourself.

1. **Become aware**. Sitting or standing in a balanced posture, bring your awareness into the inner experience you're having and acknowledge the thoughts going through your mind and the feelings going through your body at that moment.

2. **Focus on the physical sensation of the breath**. Watch and feel the movement of the abdomen rising and falling with each breath. Don't try to change the breath, just observe it as it is. When your attention wanders, guide it back gently to the breathing with your whole focus.

3. **Expand the field of awareness** around the breathing so that it includes a sense of the body as a whole. Wherever there is particular tension or discomfort, imagine the breath reaching these areas to bring a sense of relaxation and comfort. In this way you are being self-compassionate, nurturing any unpleasant sensations – healing them rather than trying to banish them.

Keep returning to the body as a whole and each breath until the pressure shifts and a more peaceful feeling ensues.

(Three Minute Meditation from *Mindfulness: A Practical Guide to Finding Peace in a Frantic World* by Professor Mark Williams and Danny Penman)

Suffering.

There is too much suffering. We have to find a way of transmuting our own suffering, anxieties, insecurities and fear into positive energy. By recognising them for what they are we take control of them and change the energy from negative to positive. And in that change-over, that transmutation, there is a spark – a powerful energy. Like the charge you feel when you hold two magnets together that don't yet touch.

If we can deal with our suffering in this way, we're well on the road to achieving inner peace.

'We let ourselves be at the mercy of our thoughts and our thoughts at the mercy of our negative emotion, in this way we undermine ourselves.'

TIBETAN SAYING
(SOURCED FROM *A Fearless Heart*
BY THUPTEN JINPA)

Even regrets can be a form of suffering. But we have to remember that where we are now, at this moment, is the sum total of all that has happened in our lives. All the decisions and experiences have led us to where we are now. If we agonise that we've missed an opportunity – in work, in love, in life – then we must also know there can no longer be regret since, for whatever reason at the time, we did not choose, or were not able, to take that particular path. We moved along.

So you see how by undoing the knots that keep regret tied up inside us we can become free of it. And from then on by applying awareness to whatever actions or decisions we take will become part of the fabric of our life. Our future circumstances and our future peace of mind will be, in part, a result of the decisions we take today.

The intangible mind is capable of healing. Even in the midst of pain we can reassure ourselves that we will recover and heal. Just as the pain of fire warns us not to physically touch it, so too the pain experienced in our mind is telling us something. Being in touch with our feelings in this way is a great strength and only through having experienced pain can we be truly compassionate beings. Perhaps, too, through being aware of the horrors of war and conflict, we can redouble our efforts towards finding peaceful solutions. Of course it would be naïve to suggest that most of us can or will achieve living in a permanent state of bliss, but we almost certainly *can* achieve a more peaceful and happy life than the one we might be living and be better equipped to cope with our responses to the natural changes in the circumstances of our lives.

A great deal of our pain remains attached to events that have happened in the past; and when these memories come to the fore we replay the pain again and again. Through mindfulness we come to accept that these events belong only in the past, and instead of experiencing a repeat of the emotional pain we can detach ourselves from that past as we get back to living in the present moment.

Remember, we have the freedom to think anything we want. If we want to end suffering and be happy it is up to us to start changing our mind; to change our thoughts and attitude and to consciously introduce more joy and gratitude into our lives.

'If you are pained by external things, it is not they that disturb you, but your own judgement of them. And it is in your power to wipe out that judgement now.'

MARCUS AURELIUS

I believe we have a baseline of joy that we constantly struggle to live on, against the tide of suffering that either we cause ourselves or we allow others to cause us. Working on dealing with our suffering will raise that baseline of joy. We all know how contagious emotions are – when we are around people who are complaining and humourless we can very easily 'catch' the emotion; and with people who express joy and laughter we can also 'catch' that. So we too can influence the atmosphere around us for the better, by living joyfully.

Seeing the world from this wider perspective, through communicating our inner peace and joy, creates a reverberation, helping us in turn to face anxiety and other uncomfortable emotions that come our way.

'*You must understand the whole of life, not just one little part of it. That is why you must read, that is why you must look at the skies, that is why you must sing and dance, and write poems, and suffer, and understand, for all that is life.*'

KRISHNAMURTI

Another area in which we can rewire our minds is in the levels of expectations we create within ourselves. When we anticipate the future result of an action of ours or someone else's, we merge our wishes, our desires, with the actual, eventual outcome. We simply cannot know what an outcome will be, since it remains in the future. So it follows that our expectations are, to a degree, fantasy. Which is why we are so often disappointed in life. This is not to say we shouldn't remain positive (in the present) and construct our plans towards what we hope might happen (in the future). We should travel hopefully, but by letting go of expectations, or at least keeping them realistic, our minds become calmer, less anxious – and more peaceful.

It's worth remembering that this internal chattering mind we are aware of is still ours – it is still 'us'. Often the chattering is dissenting, as though it is at odds with another part of us, giving rise to the feeling of having a divided self – both sides talking to each other. It is a subconscious debate between the ego and our natural instincts – our inner guiding voice. The more we can merge the two into our one whole self, the calmer our minds will be and the more peaceful and happy we will be. First, we need to make friends with ourselves.

It is a subject we can choose to think about when meditating. Simply practising being aware of a friendly, non-judgemental attitude towards ourselves, where we can eventually think and act with one voice, in one direction.

When it all gets too much and the chaos inside gets louder and louder, it's time to listen to what the body and mind needs – a rest. This could be anything from stepping outside the meeting room to get a breath of fresh air to taking a day off. An occasional 'duvet day' is like regulating the valve on a pressure cooker, preventing a build-up of steam. But the day shouldn't be frittered away in online games and watching movies, it is a chance to totally wind down the mind, to sleep, rest and give the mind the chance to recalibrate – naturally. A day of 'retreat'. Only have around you books or materials that are inspiring and motivating for your mind to take you forward, renewed and refreshed. It could also be a weekend day – although that's harder to find with a family or young children to look after, but anything's doable with a little pre-planning. If you were unwell everyone would fit in around your day in bed. You may not be unwell but you want to stay well. And as far as our peaceful state is concerned, it all starts in the mind.

What we all want at its most simple level is to be happy, to be well, to feel connected, to have peace of mind. So it is the mind more than anything that we have to clear first. Like the engine room, it's the place that has to be kept in good order and not left solely to its own devices.

'You can never get to peace and inner security without first acknowledging all the good things in your life. If you are forever wanting and longing for more without first appreciating things the way they are, you'll stay in discord.'

DOC CHILDRE AND HOWARD MARTIN
AT THE HEARTMATH INSTITUTE

Very often, when we feel we lack happiness it is because we lack awareness. When we act in a rush, without thinking, we are setting ourselves up for results from those actions that create difficulties and problems for us to deal with. The more we can act with awareness, the more we are creating peacefulness and happiness in our lives.

When you feel out of sorts, just stop what you're doing and thinking and bring your mind to the present moment. Concentrate on the simple act of your breathing and allow your mind to go with whatever you are feeling, acknowledging that it is happening, but that it will pass. Stay in this awareness and you will gradually feel a warmth envelop you, some sort of comfort and equilibrium. Having regained your internal balance, you can go forward with firmer steps again.

Mindfulness should not be thought of as a series of complicated exercises or dutiful practice. It simply means a way of applying awareness to whatever we are doing, so that we are doing, or thinking, one thing at a time and giving it our full attention – in the present moment. Even if we are planning a complicated agenda for the following month, we are constructing it in the present moment and it needs our full attention if it is to be a successful plan. Neither meditation nor mindfulness require an understanding of abstract philosophical concepts, but are activities or attitudes woven into every aspect of our daily life.

It is not *apart* from us, but *part* of us.

'When you eat, eat. When you sleep, sleep.'

BUDDHA

Little by little you will be aware of great changes in your life. As you apply mindfulness (awareness) into every aspect of your daily life you will see how it affects your relationships with other people.

Because you will be more grounded, more balanced, acting and reacting from your true self, uncluttered by constant distractions away from your awareness, you will no longer be self-conscious but confident, not unsure but sure, not muddled but articulate, not anxious but peaceful. People will react to you more directly and in response to your natural compassion towards others.

It may at first seem like an impossible task – to apply this awareness if we are not used to it. We are used, more likely, to a form of internal chaos, which permeates our outer behaviour and character. So we have a dualistic approach to everything – the person we are striving to be, the person at odds with our egotistical and selfish attitude, the dissenting voices guiding or pulling us in different directions. It's not surprising that we may go through life being anxious and far from peaceful on a daily basis. But it is not an impossible task. It may take practice to change or unscramble ingrained habits but it will happen naturally the more we become aware of our authentic self, and when (a non-dualistic) awareness becomes our new 'habit'.

Think of awareness as your light source. So if you have a train of thought or impulse that is unpleasant and you don't need to pursue it, switch it off and move over to another activity or thought process. Change the negative energy to a positive one; the force of the energy is there, the strength of the impulse remains, but we turn it into positive energy. There is no residue here. We are not trying to bury a forceful energy, we are turning it into something else. Mental alchemy.

Switching off or letting go doesn't mean suppressing thoughts or ideas but inspecting them and then deciding whether to keep them or let them go.

When negative emotions such as resentment, anger or jealousy arise we can learn to take a breath and be aware of what is happening. Not letting ourselves be carried away by them; not letting ourselves automatically justify our negative behaviour, but finding a way through which is compassionate not only towards other people but towards ourselves as well.

Practising mindfulness, meditation or awareness doesn't imply necessarily having an empty mind, but a less-full one.

Mindful not **mind full**.

There are times when it is important to think through a particular situation, behaviour or outcome. Instead of allowing thoughts to swamp you and clamour for attention, decide to select one topic and think that through with focus and awareness. By simplifying your thinking behaviour you give your inner voice a chance to be heard, to guide you in the right direction towards the best solution.

In the same way that we can train ourselves to *think* only one thought process at a time, so we can train ourselves to *do* one thing at a time. If we watch an athlete, a concert pianist, a rock-climber or an Olympic diver we can see the extremely focused awareness that they apply to what they are doing. We will be much more productive, more efficient and more successful in life if we attend to the job, the conversation, the project to hand rather than trying to do several things at once at the same time as thinking about what we will be doing later.

We become easily distracted. Try switching off the email alert on your phone or computer settings. We look at them often enough but if we hear them pinging we tend to check what has come in. Develop the habit of not replying to emails instantly, that way people don't build up an expectation (or disappointment) when you don't reply immediately. Build some peace back into your daily life. Slow down. Once we develop awareness and mindfulness as part of our practical lives – and not something that remains simply aspirational – we will discover a new type of peace of mind, a serenity and tranquillity that becomes increasingly impervious to that constant hum of anxiety.

Developing patience in our busy lives is very important. We rely on speed of communication to propel our
relationships – both business and personal. So we
become impatient for replies, impatient for results of
our endeavours. There are some things that cannot be
hurried. Look at nature to gather inspiration. Flowers
blossom when the conditions are right; fruit does not
take kindly to being forced to ripen. Nature has its own
timing despite also being in the twenty-first century.

Being close to nature cultivates the spirit of peace within us. It is one of the reasons why gardening is such a popular activity. Anyone who enjoys gardening knows the pleasure, the peaceful pleasure, in simply being outside and digging about in the earth.

Taking steps closer to nature in the wilderness takes us incrementally deeper to that peace within us. Getting off the well-beaten track is something we could all do with once in a while. How wild and for how long is up to the individual, but there is no doubt that a spell away from the urban clash gives our own peace a better chance.

Henry David Thoreau (1817–1862) was an American essayist, poet and practical philosopher. In 1845 he began his famous two-year stay on Walden Pond in Massachusetts, USA, which he wrote about in his celebrated book: *Walden*.

Thoreau's philosophy was that the more unnecessarily costly the house that people live in, the more time they need to spend working in order to earn the money to pay for it – either in mortgage or rent – setting up a constant chain of pressure and discord. So he set out to explore at what sacrifice our more advanced dwellings were obtained, by going into the woods with an axe, cutting down some trees and building himself a modest but sturdy cabin.

The enduring popularity of the book and his quest to find a simpler solution to housing and living indicates that his philosophy and way of life merits consideration. The message isn't necessarily that we all have to take to the woods and build our own cabin, but in finding a balance that works for us, and our affordability, and thus contributing largely to how peaceful a life we can have.

'The good life is one inspired by love and guided by knowledge.'

BERTRAND RUSSELL

Give your peace a chance.

Spare moments in the day are often spent habitually checking email or messages. It's good to break the constant habit. Choose instead to consciously sit, screen-free, and have a coffee, enjoying its simple pleasure, or take a walk, phone-free, to the bus stop or car park, being aware of the sights and sounds that surround you. If you have to wait for an appointment or a delayed train or plane, allow yourself a few moments to enjoy doing nothing. This all gives peace a chance to filter into your system.

Search out peaceful places that you can visit on a regular basis to get away and simply sit and breathe in some peace; to let the body and mind settle back into balance. Even in a town or city there is usually a good choice – a museum or art gallery, library, park garden, a side alcove in a church or cathedral or a plush armchair in the foyer of a large hotel.

Research buildings in your area that have been architecturally designed to promote the atmosphere of peacefulness and quiet.

Establish a range of places to suit your geography, the weather and your inclination for occasional five-minute peaceful opt-outs.

'I can't hear myself think' is a phrase we've all used at some point. It is another reason why we should actively seek out places of silence or make room for silent thinking in our busy lives.

When we listen with our spirit – our inner ear – we can eventually hear the rhythm in our heartbeat and then silence itself. It gives us a chance to 'hear ourselves think'.

We can regain a lot more control over our own dominion by spending more time with ourselves. Which is not to say that getting lost in a television programme or an online game isn't sometimes relaxing, but we all too often turn off our own switch so that we don't have to face dealing with our lives. We escape because we want to get away from ourselves – we're escaping from ourselves. Instead of always reaching for the remote control (literally and metaphorically), investing in our peace of mind will reward us with long-term joy and fulfilment compared to the quick fix of escapism.

We could think about it in the same way that sometimes we might enjoy fast food or a nutritionless snack, but for long-term good health we need the balance of a daily, healthy diet.

Festina lente – make haste slowly.

This is a good Italian phrase that people living in the fast lane should make their mantra. Slow down. Living life at a pace that truly suits you means that you stay in harmony with your own heart and mind, which in turn promotes a more peaceful life.

Caught up in urgency and demands, we are encouraged to think that we must all become masters of multi-tasking, whereas in fact by doing two or more things at once we are simply diluting the attention we give each of the tasks. Switch into the slow lane for a moment to catch your breath. Prioritise and proceed.

'Never be in a hurry; do everything quietly and in a calm spirit. Do not lose your inner peace for anything whatsoever, even if your whole world seems upset.'

SAINT FRANCIS DE SALES

Eat your way to peace.

According to the Indian-rooted practice of medicine for health and well-being – Ayurveda – there are three qualities in nature: *sattva* (serenity, compassion), *rajas* (movement, aggressiveness) and *tamas* (inertia). As with any life force, we need a combination of each of these qualities, although one is more likely to be dominant at any time. We can therefore adjust our tempo by eating food that is better suited to the pace that we need to achieve.

A sattvic diet was originally devised for the development of higher consciousness, so it is the purest of the categories. It consists of vegetarian food – food rich in life force, such as organic fresh fruit and vegetables, grains, nuts and seeds. It means avoiding tinned and processed food and selecting crops free from chemical fertilisers or sprays.

In the search for a quieter, more peaceful spell in our lives we would ideally seek to eat foods which are sattvic. These promote clarity of mind, which in turn leads to a peaceful mind.

It is beyond the scope of this book to go into the details of this particular diet, but it serves to remind us that we can change the tempo of our bodies by choosing to eat quieter food to suit the needs of our individual systems.

It is not only in Indian culture that there are references to the importance of attaining a peaceful life through our diet but also in many other cultures that have not lost knowledge of this vital tradition. From China to the Brazilian rainforests to the Mediterranean, there are pockets of lifestyle where longevity and peaceful life can go hand in hand.

There is no doubt that a peaceful digestion contributes to a peaceful life, so avoid the following:

- Eating too fast or crunched with tension.

- Overeating and drinking – overloading the system.

- Eating processed food, chemically adulterated packaged snacks, fizzy drinks, sugar-laden food and snacks.

- Overly spicy food at a time when the body needs 'quieter' food.

- Eating late in the evening and disturbing the night's sleep and rest.

- Food on the go – fast, nutritionless food.

- Eating without thinking about the food source.

- Neglecting to listen to the system to be aware as to what it wants or needs – or learning from when it is unhappy.

Treat others the way you want to be treated.

It's so simplistic a mantra that it would be easy to overlook.

But how true it is.

'My religion is simple. My religion is kindness.'

DALAI LAMA

A common thread to our invocations:

'Our fractured world is in turmoil. Mother Earth gathered all of her children into the folds of her embrace to wipe away tears. Why do you fight? You were created from male and female and made into nations and tribes so you could get to know one another and learn to coexist.'

QUR'AN, 49:13

'Our response to something we experience as an attack on civilization must spur us to deepen our personal and communal commitments to build the world from love faster than anyone can tear it down.'

RABBI MENACHEM CREDITOR,
CONGREGATION NETIVOT SHALOM
IN BERKELEY, CA

'*Shanti, Shanti, Shanti.*'

A Hindu peace prayer; each of the words Shanti – meaning peace – refers to peace in the world, the human race and our own hearts.

'*Peace I leave with you; my peace I give to you. Not as the world gives do I give to you. Let not your hearts be troubled, neither let them be afraid.*'

THE NEW TESTAMENT, JOHN 14:27

'*The giver of peace is eternally blissful.*'

SRI GURU GRANTH SAHIB

'If it is peace you want, seek to change yourself, not other people. It is easier to protect your feet with slippers than to carpet the whole of the earth.'

ANTHONY DE MELLO

Everyone needs space in which to be quiet and grow their own peace.

'Let there be spaces in your togetherness,
And let the winds of the heavens dance between
you.
Love one another but make not a bond of love:
Let it rather be a moving sea between the shores
of your souls.
Fill each other's cup but drink not from one cup.
Give one another of your bread but eat not from
the same loaf.
Sing and dance together and be joyous, but let
each one of you be alone,
Even as the strings of a lute are alone though they
quiver with the same music.
Give your hearts, but not into each other's
keeping.
For only the hand of Life can contain your hearts.
And stand together, yet not too near together:
For the pillars of the temple stand apart,
And the oak tree and the cypress grow not in each
other's shadow.'

KAHLIL GIBRAN, *The Prophet*

People who are sceptical about achieving world peace may baulk at the idea because it appears monumental in its concept, and because they cannot perceive a quick result. It is a gradual shift.

With the coming of spring not all the buds burst into leaf together but one day we look out and all the trees are green. So it is, or could be, with peace.

'Peace is a daily, a weekly, a monthly process, gradually changing opinions, slowly eroding old barriers, quietly building new structures.'

JOHN F. KENNEDY

Children need inner peace, too.

Though it's much more complex for them to recognise or be able to vocalise the lack of it. We can help children, especially young children, by listening to them and encouraging them to discuss issues of 'peace' in general. This helps in having an open-ended conversation so that if they encounter unkind or bullying behaviour from other children (or adults) they can talk about it more comfortably and with a language already accessible to them.

If adults are affected by scenes of violence on the news, how much more so are children if they see other children suffer as a result of war and conflict? It is important to have ways of addressing this and to help encourage them to make the connection between peace among countries of the world, as well as peace within family, schools and their community.

An inspiring or helpful mantra to teach children for when they are feeling muddled or conflicted is:

'.**b**'(dot be). It stands for: 'Stop, Breathe and Be!'

This is a simple maxim written by experienced classroom teachers and mindfulness practitioners to help in a wide range of contexts and ages, but particularly for schoolchildren and students. (*mindfulnessinschools. org/what-is-b)*

As children grow up we can teach them the value of developing serenity, peacefulness and compassion – along with everything else that they are taught. In the last few years mindfulness as a subject has been introduced into many schools across the world as part of the curriculum and as a way of guiding children towards the importance of inner quiet in their otherwise noisy worlds.

*'When you smile it means you have peace.
If you are angry you will never smile.'*

TOM, AGED SIX

When the opportunity presents itself, ask children to describe what they mean by 'peace'. Their answers and spontaneous associations are often enlightening.

Sometimes it is helpful for them to see that when we talk of peace it's not only about 'world peace' but how we can find it around us and inside us, and how, in that way, we are all part of creating a peaceful environment which in turn leads towards a more peaceful world. It depends on the age of the children or students but it invariably leads to an interesting exchange.

Children are still finding out for themselves the complexities of peacefulness and aggression in the playground. Teaching them how to (peacefully) resolve conflicts is of great help to them.

In a non-heated environment, talk to them about the importance of finding peaceful ways to solve arguments. Children enjoy role play so you can use this to discuss issues that might be difficult to deal with in a moment of conflict but are helpful to have put into place in quiet times. A 'peace' object can be nominated – it could be a shell or a particular book, anything that everyone is agreed on. When an argument needs to be resolved or a conflict diffused in tense situations, the children involved – and maybe adults –take turns to talk. No one may interrupt while the person holding the peace object is talking. If a child refuses to participate or if they leave the room in a temper they have effectively 'lost' the argument.

With encouragement children generally have a natural enthusiasm for sharing in the care of their environment. It is a valuable way of teaching them respect and compassion towards other living things – the universe, animals, plants – as well as their fellow beings.

'I have a dream ... that my four little children will one day live in a nation where they will not be judged by the color of their skin, but by the content of their character.'

MARTIN LUTHER KING, JR

The rainbow walk.

This is a lovely walking activity to do with a child. It is so absorbing for them that they can enter into its playfulness as well as enjoying walking with awareness.

Choose where you're going to go for a walk – there are colours everywhere and that's all that is needed. Go through the colours in the order of the rainbow and spot things that are red, then orange, yellow, green, blue and purple.

When children are relaxed and open in this way, it provides a good opportunity to begin a conversation with them about anything that might be troubling them, what is on their mind and therefore what might help them feel more peaceful.

Or simply to enjoy a way of walking and talking and observing together.

The pebble talk.

This is a simple mindfulness or awareness activity to do quietly with children to help them cultivate ways of being peaceful within, so they can be peaceful in the world.

It can be done anywhere with either one or many children.

Each child is given a small bag and four pebbles. Or they can find their own bag and pebbles. If they enjoy the activity you can then keep the favourite pebbles in the bag and practise the exercise more often. And going for a walk on the beach can have the added purpose for them of looking for their meditation pebbles.

One by one the pebbles are given an image to relate to.

- The first is a beautiful flower that they can imagine. The flower represents freshness and fragile beauty.

- The second is of a mountain that is solid and firm no matter what is going on around it.

- The third is still water in a lake – for clarity and calmness.

- The fourth is the spacious blue sky for freedom – feeling free from worry and anxiety.

(Adapted with kind permission from *A Handful of Quiet*, Thich Nhat Hanh, Plum Blossom Books)

Keep the peace.

- Bring the concept of peace into focus so that it is embedded in your daily dealings with people.

- If you are part of a family or school, propose one day a week or a month that is Peace Day.

- Watch documentaries or videos that highlight peace stories and compassion in areas of conflict or disaster.

- Make peace offerings to friends or colleagues with whom there is disagreement. These can be either verbal or in the form of a symbolic gift – perhaps an olive branch or a small olive plant, or even a jar of olives!

- Remember, you can agree to disagree peacefully.

Achieving more peace in the world will be brought about not solely by marching on demonstrations and signing petitions but as much through our capacity for showing compassion, being peaceful and living an authentic life. Through consciously making at least one peaceful act a day we can contribute to world peace in the global community as effectively as any politician.

'*A peace is of the nature of a conquest;*
For then both parties nobly are subdued,
And neither party loser.'

WILLIAM SHAKESPEARE,
Henry IV, Part 2, Act 4, Scene 2

Human nature is such that it is proud and does not like to lose face. That's why a good peace strategy in war or an argument will include a solution that allows the other party to climb down from an indefensible opinion or position without coercion.

Despite our individual characters, ultimately everything and everyone is connected, not disconnected or detached, and as such we must work together on a course towards a solution for peaceful living – for survival and not destruction.

'If a drop of water happens to fall into an ocean, some part of that water will remain, as long as that ocean remains; left on its own, that drop of water will just dry up.'

BUDDHIST SAYING

Ashoka Maurya (304–232 BCE), considered one of India's greatest emperors, went through an extraordinary transition from being warmonger to peacemaker. After witnessing the mass deaths of the biggest war of his campaigns – the Kalinga war, in which hundreds of thousands of people were killed and displaced in order for Ashoka to conquer the state – he turned to Buddhism. Out of remorse and dismay at the death and devastation that war had inflicted on human beings – and the animal and vegetable world – Ashoka not only continued to be a strong and powerful leader but converted to negotiations through non-violence. His empire continued to flourish and has been described as one of the few instances in world history where a government has made provision for the protection, well-being and moral welfare of animals as well as the human populace.

What is interesting about this piece of history is that a bloodthirsty warmonger could change so radically in denouncing weapons of destruction to govern in a peaceful, non-violent manner. He arrived at the teaching of peace through his inner sense of remorse and futility at seeing the effects of war and destruction.

It is inspiring to be reminded of examples where global leaders – men and women of distinction – have managed to overcome conflict in favour of peace.

Remorse can be an important instigator in regulating our own behaviour. It is a form of positive awareness because it often leads to inner peace when it has been redressed. Suffering remorse for an action we have made shows that there is, within us, a sense of compassion. An important building block with which to create a foundation for peace.

Some 2,000 years after Ashoka's denunciation of violent means, Nelson Mandela was dramatically altering his view on the use of force to achieve solutions. In the 1960s Mandela became part of the armed wing of the African National Congress, advocating the use of violence in order to overthrow the South African apartheid regime. Ultimately, the world remembers Mandela not for his call to arms but for his gentler call for reconciliation in a country deeply divided by race, and for his part in negotiating a peaceful end to apartheid.

'Nelson Mandela went to jail believing in violence, and 27 years later he and his colleagues had slowly and carefully honed the skills, the incredible skills, that they needed to turn one of the most vicious governments the world has known into a democracy. And they did it in a total devotion to non-violence.'

SCILLA ELWORTHY

'Every government has as much of a duty to avoid war as a ship's captain has to avoid a shipwreck.'

GUY DE MAUPASSANT

In charge of our thoughts.

All too often we become hostage to our thoughts – as though they control us. They don't, or rather, they needn't. Practising awareness with the objective of achieving inner peace will gradually tip the balance to a point where we are in charge of our minds and our thoughts, not the other way round.

*'I am determined to be cheerful and happy
in whatever situation I may find myself. For
I have learned that the greater part of our
misery or unhappiness is determined not by our
circumstance but by our disposition.'*

MARTHA WASHINGTON

In case we forget . . .

For some people, having affirmations that they relate to are helpful in replacing negative thoughts with positive ones.

Choose your own affirmations; write them on cards and dot them around the house, on the refrigerator, the bathroom mirror, in the car, on your computer at work. Change the affirmations once in a while or move them around so that your brain doesn't just read them and not let them filter through.

Time out.

This exercise can be done at home (or possibly in the office!) anytime we need to regain our balance.

Lie flat on the floor, feet slightly elevated on a cushion so that they are higher than your head. Do nothing for a few moments while your thoughts gambol around, until they settle and your heartbeat slows. Then focus on your breathing to stop the mind chattering. Just go with the breath in and out, gradually letting it find its natural rhythm. We don't look at the waves breaking on the foreshore and think they are too fast or too slow, they are always at the right pace for what they do. We must learn to do the same in order to feel peaceful.

When the internal chatter gets in the way of peace, stop and listen to the outer sounds around you. They might be peaceful, mellow sounds like waves breaking or birdsong, but they might also be discordant sounds that you can't shut out – traffic noise, horns, sirens, other people's voices. Yet you can still consciously listen to the sounds and by being aware of them, focusing on them, you are distracted from the constant scrabble of words and thoughts in your mind. By closing your eyes you are gradually even able to hear the silence between the various noises and find pockets of unexpected peace.

Music is made up not just of notes but as much by the space between them.

Strive to be happy.

Easy to say when we are feeling relatively upbeat, but difficult to access when we are feeling sad or depressed. Somehow, though, by developing our *desire* for peace, that striving is rewarded. Feeling at peace is a form of being happy. From that renewed basis, happiness in other ways seems more attainable. We don't have to be ecstatic to be happy, we simply need to be peaceful.

'Happiness is when what you think, what you say and what you do are in harmony.'

MAHATMA GANDHI

There are many things we think we want or need or desire to make us happy – desiderata.

Desiderata

Go placidly amid the noise and haste, and remember what peace there may be in silence.

As far as possible, without surrender, be on good terms with all persons.

Speak your truth quietly and clearly and listen to others, even the dull and ignorant; they too have their story.

Avoid loud and aggressive persons, they are vexatious to the spirit.

If you compare yourself with others, you may become vain and bitter, for always there will be greater and lesser persons than yourself.

Enjoy your achievements as well as your plans. Keep interested in your career, however humble; it is a real possession in the changing fortunes of time.

Exercise caution in your business affairs; for the world is full of trickery.

But let this not blind you to what virtue there is; many persons strive for high ideals and everywhere life is full of heroism.

Be yourself.

Especially, do not feign affection.

Neither be critical about love, for in the face of all aridity and disenchantment it is as perennial as the grass.

Take kindly the counsel of the years, gracefully surrendering the things of youth.

Nurture strength of spirit to shield you in sudden misfortune. But do not distress yourself with imaginings. Many fears are born of fatigue and loneliness. Beyond a wholesome discipline, be gentle with yourself.

You are a child of the universe, no less than the trees and the stars, you have a right to be here. And whether or not it is clear to you, no doubt the universe is unfolding as it should. Therefore be at peace with God, whatever you conceive Him to be, and whatever your labors and aspirations, in the noisy confusion of life keep peace with your soul. With all its sham, drudgery and broken dreams, it is still a beautiful world. Be careful. Strive to be happy.

Attributed to both Max Ehrmann, the American poet born in 1872, and an inscription found in Old Saint Paul's Church, Baltimore, Maryland, in 1692.

'If more of us valued food and good cheer and song above hoarded gold, it would be a merrier world.'

J.R.R. TOLKEIN

Being – just being not doing – is an important part of our daily lives. This doesn't mean switching off (necessarily) but being aware of the moment that you're in. Initially this practice gives us a feeling of 'watching' ourselves 'be'. But after a while, the watcher and the watched merge, as we become integrated in the present moment, being alert, being mindful – just being.

'*A culture of peace and non-violence goes to the substance of fundamental human rights: social justice, democracy, literacy, respect and dignity for all, international solidarity, respect for workers' rights and core labour standards, children rights, equality between men and women, cultural identity and diversity, indigenous peoples and minorities' rights, humane behaviour towards animals and the preservation of the natural environment.*'

EDUCATION INTERNATIONAL

'If the human race wishes to have a prolonged and indefinite period of material prosperity, they have only got to behave in a peaceful and helpful way towards one another.'

WINSTON CHURCHILL

It is good to be aware of the natural forces and opportunities available for us to utilise. It gives inspiration a chance to be heard so we can implement new ideas. In the same way that a surfer knows how to read the weather, the wind, the wave, to harness herself to its power, we can, with perception, make the most of conditions and circumstances that surround us. Only a peaceful mind can enjoy that clarity of discernment, knowing when to let go and knowing when to go with the flow of life. So it is important to have peace – for its own sake but also in order to keep the mind open to opportunity and change.

'You can't stop the waves, but you can learn to surf.'

JON KABAT–ZINN

In Lao Tzu's chronicle *Tao Te Ching*, one of his teachings (23) talks of knowing when to stop and when to continue along the way.

> *'Express yourself completely,*
> *then keep quiet.*
> *Be like the forces of nature:*
> *when it blows, there is only wind;*
> *when it rains, there is only rain;*
> *when the clouds pass, the sun shines through.'*

And the verse ends:

'... *trust your natural responses*
and everything will fall into place.'

Knowing when to stop or pull back is an important skill to hone.

We stop eating when our hunger is satisfied, or drinking when our thirst is slaked. If we eat or drink beyond that point we feel nauseous, unwell, even regretful. We can practise knowing when to stop in many different ways each day: when to stop talking, resting, complaining, eating, drinking, demanding, and more.

Another benefit of knowing when to stop is experiencing a softening in our attitude and behaviour. We become more flexible, open to spontaneity and joy, going with the flow of life.

We tend to accumulate problems. Worrying has become endemic even to people already living in a privileged society of freedom, relative wealth, access to health care and security. If we learn to accept the things we cannot control, and if we have our foundation of inner peace to build upon, then we can start reducing the worry factor. How often have we worried about something only to discover that the outcome was not as bad as we had anticipated? And that, before long, we look around for something else to worry about? Worrying is a habit that can gradually be curbed – starting with a shift in attitude.

Reducing worry in our lives – habitual worry – will allow peace to grow. Once you've had a taste of inner peace – not just fleetingly but as part of your life – you will be eager to have more of it. When you feel a sense of joy gradually become your gold standard, you will find that happiness has come to you rather than being at the end of an interminable quest. And it can begin by actively eradicating much of our worry time.

I like the advice from Dr Ad Kerkhof, Professor of Clinical Psychology at the VU University, Amsterdam, who specialises in worry and depression.

For any of us plagued by worry he suggests factoring in two 'worry slots' a day. This way they aren't squashed and ignored, just tamed and scheduled. The 'worry slots' shouldn't be taken in a comfortable chair or lying in bed but at a desk or table – dealing with them as we would any other task that has to be done. The fifteen-minute slots can be marked in the diary or programmed into our smartphone calendars.

'Nature abhors a vacuum.' It's as though anxiety is constantly waiting in the wings for a vacuum to be created in our minds or thoughts into which it will rush. If, however, we plant a 'groundcover' of inner peace, then the weeds of worry won't be able to take root.

More weeds to clear.

To criticise, to always expect the worst, to dislike someone or some place before we've even met them or been there are all negative traits that are a barrier to inner peace. However, these can be eliminated once we know they are simply bad habits that have accumulated to the point that we hardly notice them any more. Once we do this, once we shine awareness on them, we can start doing something about it.

We need to replace these weeds with a healthy balance between focusing on others and focusing on ourselves. This way, we do not fall into either of the two extremes of obsessive care-giving or excessive self-preoccupation.

Gratitude.

Opening ourselves up to gratitude is a major first step out of negativity. Gratitude is basically expressing appreciation for what we have, as opposed to expressing dissatisfaction for what we do not. It increases positive energy through a more enduring level of happiness or contentment with what we count ourselves fortunate in having, rather than the negative sense of 'longing' or 'desiring' (especially in a material, consumer-driven interpretation).

Forgiveness.

We can always find ways to justify our sense of entitlement in holding back forgiveness towards someone. Our view on the situation may be so biased that we are incapable of taking a fair and balanced position. But in taking steps towards a peaceful, more harmonious life, practising being non-judgemental is fundamental. Take a few breaths; stand back from the problem to give it some space and understanding. Forgive and move on, carrying a lighter load with which to travel. Resentment only weighs us down and slows us up.

Compassion.

Behaving towards others as we would like to be treated ourselves gives us a basic blueprint of how to engage with people. So often we act – or react – *automatically*, without thinking consciously of our behaviour and its consequences. By practising peacefulness we can monitor our behaviour, and in so doing we are more likely to be mindful of other people's needs for help or comfort in times of difficulty.

'Never criticise anyone until you have walked for two weeks in his moccasins.'

NATIVE AMERICAN PROVERB

Mencius, the Chinese philosopher (*c.* 372–289 BCE), asserted that the individual's innate goodness was challenged by society's lack of a positive cultivating influence arrived at by greed, envy and laziness. He nominated the three virtues of the individual by which to live a rich and peaceful life as wisdom, compassion and courage.

'He who exerts his mind to the utmost knows his nature,' and, 'The way of learning is none other than finding the lost mind.'

WING-TSIT CHAN (TRANS.), 1963,
A Source Book in Chinese Philosophy

Imagine having more times in your life when you have less unease and concerns – pretty much whatever the circumstances – where you experience a calmness, a peacefulness. It is achievable. One of the keys to accessing this state is developing the ability to deal with things as they arise.

If a thought comes into your head that troubles you, or a situation presents itself that is unsatisfactory, then instead of abandoning yourself to be the victim of either the thought or circumstance, take control of your mind.

Look at the choices and remember the maxim: either *accept* it, *alter* it, or *let go of it*. Even if events continue to be troublesome, if you have applied one of the choices then you will have risen above the situation. Not in a submissive way, but because that is your only choice until you can apply another of the solutions.

'Until he extends the circle of his compassion to all living things, man will not himself find peace.'

ALBERT SCHWEITZER (1875–1965)

Irrespective of a religious, spiritual or secular life, and irrespective of race or culture, peace of mind is an aspiration that everyone belonging to the human race has, to a greater or lesser degree. And peace of mind in turn leads outwards to peace in the community. The community is no longer restricted to the people we are physically surrounded by but, via the Internet, to the widest community the world has ever known.

'We live now in a global village and we are in one single family. It's our responsibility to bring friendship and love from all different places around the world and to live together in peace.'

JACKIE CHAN

Universal ethics of compassion, tolerance and loving kindness may have been central to all the world's major religions yet we are instinctively guided, driven or inspired by those same moral values by which we live or strive to live without necessarily having had a religious upbringing. So a more peaceful world is one where individual ethics are recognised as also being universal ones.

Since one of the definitions of nirvana is 'peace', it follows that millions of people are on a quest for peace – both inner and outer, and, through the idea of secularised religion, it is becoming more accessible to those without a traditional religion. The Dalai Lama says: 'We need an approach to ethics which makes no recourse to religion and can be equally acceptable to those with faith and those without: secular ethics.'

Ultimately we are all responsible for our own lives – how we live and how we die. We can't be dissidents from ourselves. If we feel a discord within us, a schism, it is usually because we are split in our desire to do something that is not in accord with our inner values and so it disturbs our inner peace.

When we start to trust more in the process of life, in the unfolding of situations towards a harmonious result or outcome, we will enjoy a new confidence and a more relaxed way of living.

Without forcing anything to happen, observe how often things do work out seemingly of their own accord once they are mindfully set in motion.

'The first peace, which is the most important, is that which comes within the souls of people when they realise their relationship, their oneness, with the universe and all its powers, and when they realise that at the centre of the universe dwells the Great Spirit, and that this centre is really everywhere, it is within each of us.

This is the real peace, and the others are but reflections of this.

The second peace is that which is made between two individuals, and the third is that which is made between two nations.

But above all you should understand that there can never be peace between nations until there is known that true peace, which, as I have often said, is within the souls of men.'

BLACK ELK, MEDICINE MAN
AND HOLY MAN OF THE OGLALA
LAKOTA (SIOUX). (1863–1950)

Paul Ekman, the American psychologist and pioneer in the study of emotions, is not alone in his belief that what he calls 'global compassion' is the most important challenge of our time.

If we, as individuals and together as a global society, can further our understanding of compassion and be motivated from that part of our nature, then we have a real chance of making a more humane world.

*'Just as I feel happy when others wish me well,
and feel touched when others show concern for my
pain and sorrow – so everyone else feels the same
way. Therefore I shall rejoice in others' happiness
and feel concerned for their pain and sorrow.'*

THUPTEN JINPA

Very often we are uncertain why we feel an inner uneasiness or disquiet. Once we start being aware that we can tap into our instinctive direction, we can discover why peaceful feelings elude us and start focusing on how to access them.

It is often out of thoughtlessness (lack of awareness) that people are selfish, bad-mannered or lacking in compassion towards others. Within ourselves, the remedy is a matter of cultivating this conscious awareness habit and practising compassion and thoughtfulness.

'I believe all suffering is caused by ignorance. People inflict pain on others in the selfish pursuit of their happiness or satisfaction. Yet true happiness comes from a sense of peace and contentment, which in turn must be achieved through the cultivation of altruism, of love and compassion, and elimination of ignorance, selfishness and greed.'

DALAI LAMA

Peaceful night ...

We are all happier and perform better when we've had a good night's sleep. And there is almost always room for improvement in preparing for sleep, including some of the following:

On evenings in, switch off the phone and run a soothing bath to soak in.

In bed and just before sleep, lie for a while on your back, stretched out but relaxed.

Reflect on your day. Briefly review the events of the day – not dwelling on things that didn't go your way but moving on to the sequence of events simply to record them and see how they match up with the intentions you made before getting up that morning.

Put your hand on your stomach – it should rise as you breathe in and fall as you breathe out.

Count your blessings.

If you have trouble getting to sleep, recall a picture of somewhere you've been that made you feel happy and relaxed. Concentrate on all the senses that contributed to that relaxed feeling. Or imagine somewhere completely new and add in all the visual and sound effects you would like.

Or, count each out breath. When your mind wanders, return to the count of one and start again. Continue this way until you fall asleep.

'If, when relaxed completely, one observes what happens, this very act in itself produces strength.'

JETSUN MILAREPA,
TIBETAN POET AND SAGE (1052–1135)

Hoping for world peace may not be an impossible ideal. Certainly there are those that agree it could happen. Surely it must follow that if everyone were to understand the power of peace of mind and practise active peace through developing their inner values, their mindful attitude, their compassion and their humanity, the world would be a more peaceful one?

In his research into the history of violence and humanity, Steven Pinker, Professor of Psychology at Harvard University, shows that today, despite what the news seems to constantly tell us, and surprising though it may be to learn, we may be living in the most peaceful time in our species' history; that violence of all kinds has been decreasing. In the title of his book, *The Better Angels of Our Nature*, Pinker uses a metaphor for four human motivations: *empathy, self-control, moral sense* and *reason*. These, he says, can 'orient us away from violence and towards cooperation and altruism'.

'Peace may sound simple – one beautiful word – but it requires everything we have, every quality, every strength, every dream, every high ideal.'

YEHUDI MENUHIN

We can begin our own peace campaign right now, right here. It requires no form filling, no allegiances, no meetings; it simply requires us to begin; to make that commitment – inner and outer. Be part of the link. Be in it, not out of it.

And remember Goethe's words:

'Whatever you can do, or dream you can do, begin it. Boldness has genius, power and magic in it. Begin it now.'

If one currency could encircle the world, let it be compassion. It is within every human being's capacity to be kind and compassionate to his or her fellow being. A thought, a word or a kind act expressed between people in their families and communities costs nothing, demands nothing.

The world is made up of individuals and their communities. So world peace becomes not one enormous barrier to tackle, but many smaller ones within our grasp.

We can all make that change.

Imagine.

'Be the change you wish to see in the world.'

MAHATMA GANDHI

Bibliography

After Buddhism, Stephen Batchelor (Yale University Press, 2015)

Anthropology and Modern Life, Franz Boas (Dover Publications Inc., 1962)

A Source Book in Chinese Philosophy, Wing-Tsit Chan (Princeton University Press, 1963)

Beyond Religion, His Holiness the Dalai Lama (Rider, 2013)

Be Here Now, Ram Dass (Dr Richard Alpert) (Crown Publications, 1978)

Gut, Giulia Enders (Scribe Publications, 2014)

A Handful of Quiet, Thich Nhat Hanh (Plum Blossom Books, 2012)

An Autobiography: The Story of My Experiments with Truth, Mahatma Gandhi (Penguin Books, 1929)

The Prophet, Kahlil Gibran (Heinemann, 1926)

A Fearless Heart, Thupten Jinpa (Piatkus, 2015)

Freedom, Love, and Action, Jiddu Krishnamurti (Shambhala Publications, 1994)

Awareness, Anthony de Mello (Fount, 1990)

Tao Te Ching, Lao Tzu

The Better Angels of Our Nature, Steven Pinker (Penguin Books, 2012)

Letters to a Young Poet, Rainer Maria Rilke (W.W. Norton, 1929)

Taming the Tiger, Akong Tulku Rinpoche (Rider, 1994)

Zen Flesh, Zen Bones, Nyogen Senzaki and Paul Reps (Anchor Books, 1957)

How Nonviolent Struggle Works, Gene Sharp (The Albert Einstein Institution, 2013)

Travels With a Donkey in the Cévennes, Robert Louis Stevenson (Chatto & Windus, 1879)

The Mystic Garden, Douglas Swinscow (The Halsgrove Press, 1992)

Walden, Henry David Thoreau (Dover Publications Inc., 1854)

Mindfulness: Finding Peace in a Frantic World, Mark Williams and Dr Danny Penman (Piatkus, 2011)

Quotes from *The Little Book of Peace* are taken from

Marcus Aurelius was a Roman emperor and the writer of Stoic philosophy.

Black Elk was a Native American medicine and holy man of the Sioux tribe.

Dr Franz Uri Boas was a German-American anthropologist and a pioneer of modern anthropology.

Jackie Chan is a Hong Kong martial artist, director, actor and producer.

Doc Childre and Howard Martin are the co-founders of the HeartMath Institute, which seeks to help people bridge the connection between their hearts and minds.

Winston Churchill was the British prime minister during the war years of 1940–1945 and again in 1951–1955.

Confucius was a Chinese teacher and philosopher in the fifth century BCE.

Rabbi Menachem Creditor is the rabbi of Congregation Netivot Shalom in Berkeley, CA.

His Holiness the Dalai Lama is the 14th Dalai Lama and spiritual leader of Tibetan Buddhism.

Max Ehrmann was an American poet, best known for his poem 'Desiderata'.

Scilla Elworthy is a peace builder and founder of the Oxford Research Group. She has been nominated three times for the Nobel Peace Price.

Indira Gandhi was India's first female prime minister.

Mahatma Gandhi was the primary leader of the Indian independence movement in British-ruled India and celebrated for his commitment to non-violent principles.

Siddartha Gautama was a sage who became known as Buddha (meaning one who is awake) and on whose teachings Buddhism was founded. He was born in India in the sixth century BCE.

Kahlil Gibran was a Lebanese-American poet, best known for his book *The Prophet*.

Johann Wolfgang von Goethe was a German poet, playwright and novelist and is widely regarded as the greatest German literary figure of the modern era.

Vincent van Gogh is one of the most well-known Post-Impressionist painters.

Dag Hammarskjold was a Swedish diplomat and was the second Secretary General of the United Nations.

Thupten Jinpa has been the principal English translator to the Dalai Lama and is the author of *A Fearless Heart*.

Jon Kabat-Zinn is the founding director of the Stress Reduction Clinic and the Center for Mindfulness in Medicine, Health Care and Society at the University of Massachusetts.

John F. Kennedy was the 35th president of the United States of America.

Martin Luther King, Jr was the leader of the African-American Civil Rights Movement.

Krishnamurti was an Indian speaker on matters that concerned humankind.

Lao Tzu was a philosopher of ancient China and author of *Tao Te Ching*.

Guy de Maupassant was a French writer particularly celebrated for his short stories.

Anne O'Hare McCormick was a journalist for the *New York Times* and is best known for her foreign news reporting during the Second World War.

Anthony de Mello was an Indian Jesuit priest, teacher and psychotherapist.

Yehudi Menuhin was an American-born violinist.

Jetsun Milarepa was a Tibetan yogi and poet in the eleventh and twelfth centuries.

Bertrand Russell was a British philosopher and peace activist.

Saint Francis de Sales was a bishop of Geneva and is honoured as a saint of the Roman Catholic Church. He is the patron saint of writers and journalists.

Albert Schweitzer was a French-German theologian, musician, physician and philosopher. He received the Nobel Peace Prize in 1952.

William Shakespeare was an English poet, actor and playwright and is considered one of the greatest writers in the English language.

Spinoza was a Dutch philosopher and is considered to have laid the groundwork for the eighteenth-century Enlightenment.

Robert Louis Stevenson was a Scottish writer, best known for *Treasure Island*, *The Strange Case of Dr Jekyll and Mr Hyde* and *Travels with a Donkey in the Cévennes*.

Mother Teresa was an Albanian Roman Catholic religious sister who founded the Missionaries of Charity.

J.R.R. Tolkein was a major scholar of the English language, specialising in Old and Middle English and best known for his books *The Hobbit* and *The Lord of the Rings*.

Martha Washington was the wife of George Washington, the first president of the United States.

Professor Mark Williams and Danny Penman are the authors of *Mindfulness: A Practical Guide to Finding Peace in a Frantic World*.